The Story of a Lifetime

A Keepsake of Personal Memoirs

Lives of great men all remind us
We can make our lives sublime,
And, departing, leave behind us
Footprints on the sands of time;

Footprints that perhaps another,
Sailing o'er life's solemn main,
A forlorn and shipwrecked brother,
Seeing, shall take heart again.

Henry Wadsworth Longfellow

THE STORY OF A LIFETIME
A Keepsake of Personal Memoirs

by

Pamela and Stephen Pavuk

Dedicated to Mary and W. E. Clyde

"Your true legacy cannot be touched, but will be felt forever."

Published by TriAngel Publishers, Inc.
Voice: 1-877-313-1444 or 1-800-579-1869. Facsimile: 1-888-874-2643.
Website: www.thestoryofalifetime.com

Plum color matte-finish laminated cover, ISBN 0-9700626-8-0.
Copyright © 2000 by TriAngel Publishers, Inc.

Green color foil-stamped leatherette cover, ISBN 0-9700626-9-9.
Copyright © 2000 by TriAngel Publishers, Inc.

Burgundy color Deluxe Edition foil-stamped genuine leather cover, ISBN 0-9700626-0-5.
Copyright © 2000 by TriAngel Publishers, Inc.

Twenty-first printing. Previous editions copyrighted in 1995, 1996 and 1997.

All original artistic illustrations (illustrations Copyright © 2000 by TriAngel Publishers, Inc.) within this publication by J. Richard Huxen, a graphic artist specializing in pen and ink, airbrush, watercolor and digital mixed media. The artist may be contacted at www.indigographicdesign.com, or by contacting the publisher.

Original artistic painting on cover by Diana Thurmon, a Georgia artist
who works in acrylic, watercolor, pastels, and pen and ink.
Her works are included in collections throughout the United States.
The artist may be contacted at Images Unlimited, 1516 Annapolis Way,
Grayson, Georgia 30017, by calling 770-979-4797, or by contacting the publisher.

All rights reserved. Except for brief excerpts quoted in reviews, no part of
the contents of this book may be reproduced by any means or in any form
without the express written permission of the publisher.

Printed and bound in the United States of America.

To everything there is a season,
A time for every purpose under heaven:
A time to be born, and a time to die;
A time to plant, and a time to pluck what is planted;
A time to kill, and a time to heal;
A time to break down, and a time to build up;
A time to weep, and a time to laugh;
A time to mourn, and a time to dance;
A time to cast away stones, and a time to gather stones;
A time to embrace, and a time to refrain from embracing;
A time to gain, and a time to lose;
A time to keep, and a time to throw away;
A time to tear, and a time to sew;
A time to keep silence, and a time to speak;
A time to love, and a time to hate;
A time of war, and a time of peace.

Ecclesiastes 3:1-8

The Story of a Lifetime

The Personal Memoirs of

_____

Table of Contents

Introduction	9
Family Background	10
Childhood	42
Teen Years	70
Higher Education	100
Military	114
Independence, Work and Career	128
Love and Marriage	146
Parenthood	164
Middle Years	190
Golden Years	204
Ethnic Heritage	220
Regrets, Mistakes, Milestones, and Turning Points	236
Beliefs, Values, Lessons and Advice	262
How Life Has Changed	288
Now	304
Favorites	320
Special Questions	330
Continuation Pages	341
Family Tree	366
Favorite Photographs and Mementos	372

*Men in their generations
are like the leaves of the trees.
The wind blows and one year's leaves
are scattered on the ground;
but the trees burst into bud
and put on fresh ones
when the spring comes round.*

Homer

Introduction

We all have stories worth sharing – of love and happiness, pain and sorrow. Too often the things we take for granted in each other are never discussed and then fade from our memory. Too late we realize there was so much more we wanted to know or wanted to tell. *The Story of a Lifetime* is designed to help you write the story of your life. It is a place for you to record the most significant events in your life, along with your unique perspective, and preserve them for those who love you and want to know you better. Your story in your own hand, in your own words, in your own "voice", will be cherished for generations.

Many questions in this book ask about your personal experiences, observations and philosophies. Answer and date those you feel are appropriate. In the chapter entitled "Special Questions", add questions (and answers) of your own to those that may have been included there by the person(s) who gave you this book, if you received it as a gift. The chapter called "Continuation Pages" is provided for any of your answers that extend beyond the space available after each question. Also included is a chapter in which your "Favorite Photographs and Mementos" can be cross-indexed to pertinent answers.

Allowing these questions to help you unfold the path you have taken in your life will enable you and others to gain some insight into the choices you made along the way. You are the subject. This is your view of things, your version of events. Some of the questions may not be easy to answer. By telling your true life story, you will likely confront painful memories as well as happy and exciting ones. All these experiences are meaningful because they have made you into who you are today.

The story of your life is so important to those who love and respect you. Your care in relating your memories and insights will long be valued and treasured. Whether you found this book on your own or received it as a gift, the true gift will be complete only when you have shared your story... *The Story of a Lifetime*.

Family Background

Throughout our lives, the institution of family is our strongest support system. Whatever satisfaction we derive from living generally arises from, has an impact on, or otherwise relates to our family situation.

More often than not, old family stories are lost and forgotten forever because they are not written down. Sadly, the thoughts and feelings of our predecessors are usually not shared for the benefit of posterity. Most of us live without a sense of deep roots. We know little about our ancestors or their experiences. Our ignorance is chiefly from simple inattention to family heritage, even though in the ways that we think, speak, act and generally live our lives, we are the genetic, cultural and social products of our ancestors, whatever their makeup may have been.

The preservation of your personal remembrances of your family in a historical context enhances appreciation of their lives and understanding of them as human beings. Your reflections about them honor them much more than simple, impersonal entries in the family tree. Perhaps more importantly, your descendants can benefit greatly from your personal observations of events surrounding your family.

We all come from the past,
and children ought to know
what it was that went into their making,
to know that life is a
braided cord of humanity
stretching up from time long gone,
and that it cannot be defined
by the span of a single journey
from diaper to shroud.

Russell Baker

If your ancestors emigrated from another country, from where did they come? When? How did they come? Where did they settle and why?

What do you remember about your oldest relative(s) you knew personally?

When and where were your mother's mother and father born? What was her mother's maiden name?

_____
_____
_____
_____
_____
_____
_____
_____
_____
_____
_____
_____

Describe the kind of persons they were.

_____
_____
_____
_____
_____
_____
_____
_____
_____
_____
_____
_____

If you have inherited any of the characteristics of your mother's parents, describe what they are and how you feel about them.

_____

What do you know about their values, philosophies and religious beliefs?

_____

What kind of work did your mother's parents do?

What else would you like to say about them?

When and where were your father's mother and father born? What was his mother's maiden name?

Describe the kind of persons they were.

If you have inherited any of the characteristics of your father's parents, describe what they are and how you feel about them.

_____
_____
_____
_____
_____
_____
_____
_____
_____
_____
_____
_____
_____

What do you know about their values, philosophy, and religious beliefs?

_____
_____
_____
_____
_____
_____
_____
_____
_____
_____
_____
_____
_____

What kind of work did your father's parents do?

What else would you like to say about them?

Has your mother shared any stories she knew about her parents' childhoods?

_____
_____
_____
_____
_____
_____
_____
_____
_____
_____
_____
_____
_____
_____
_____
_____
_____

When and where was your mother born? Where did she grow up? What was her maiden name?

_____
_____
_____
_____
_____
_____
_____
_____

Tell about the family in which your mother grew up. Do you know what her childhood was like? Do you remember any stories she told you about it?

Who ran to help me when I fell
And would some pretty story tell,
Or kiss the place to make it well?
My mother.

Jane Taylor

What memories do you have of your mother during your childhood?

Describe your mother's work, both in and out of the home.

What other interests did she have? What were her hobbies and what did she do for fun?

Which of your mother's physical and personality characteristics did you inherit?

Describe her best qualities.

Describe your mother's traits with which you are least compatible.

Did she experience much sadness or tragedy while you were little? How did she deal with it?

What is the happiest memory you have of your mother?

What is the most painful memory you have of her?

Tell about your mother's spiritual or religious beliefs.

If she is deceased, how and when did she die? Where is she buried?

What are the most important things you learned from your mother?

What else do you remember about her?

Has your father shared any stories he knew about his parents' childhoods?

When and where was your father born? Where did he grow up?

Tell about the family in which your father grew up. Do you know what his childhood was like? Do you remember any stories he told you about it?

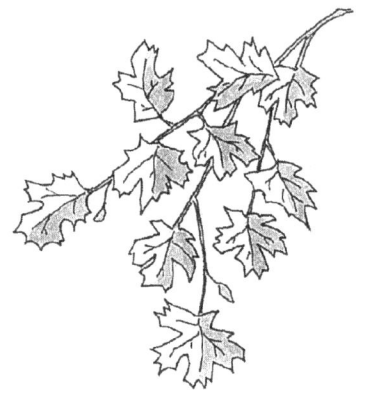

*Other things may change us,
but we start and end with the family.*

Anthony Brandt

What memories do you have of your father during your childhood?

What kind of work did your father do?

___

What other interests did he have? What were his hobbies and what did he do for fun?

Which of your father's physical and personality characteristics did you inherit?

Describe his best qualities.

Describe your father's traits with which you are least compatible.

Did he experience much sadness or tragedy while you were little? How did he deal with it?

What is the happiest memory you have of your father?

___

What is the most painful memory you have of him?

___

Tell about your father's spiritual or religious beliefs.

If he is deceased, how and when did he die? Where is he buried?

What are the most important things you learned from your father?

What else do you remember about him?

How did your mother and father meet? How long did they know each other before getting married? What do you know about their courtship and wedding?

What was their relationship like?

Does your family have any history of a particular illness, disease, genetic problem, or addiction that could be passed on from generation to generation?

_____
_____
_____
_____
_____
_____
_____
_____
_____
_____
_____
_____

Does your family have any family myths or traditions?

_____
_____
_____
_____
_____
_____
_____
_____
_____
_____

Childhood

During our early childhood, we were constantly involved in the process of learning how to cope with our ever-changing outer environment, as well as with our inner self. We observed everything that happened around us and formed our own conclusions and opinions based on what we saw and heard, thus setting a course for our own behavior.

Most instrumental were our relationships with our parents and siblings. Social, economic, religious and other factors also greatly influenced our development, but primarily it was the values, traditions and mores within the context of our immediate family which had a profound impact on whom we became and how we viewed the world.

Your most vivid memories of your childhood, both within and outside your immediate family, probably outline the framework of your personality. Your social interactions with new friends, your early school experiences, and your reactions to all the new circumstances and events in your then-expanding world are fascinating markers on the early part of your journey toward self-identity.

What the mother sings to the cradle goes all the way down to the coffin.

Henry Ward Beecher

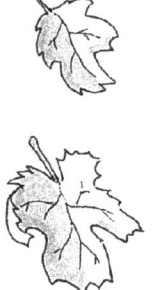

When and where were you born?

_____
_____
_____
_____
_____
_____

Was there anything unusual about your birth?

_____
_____
_____
_____
_____
_____

Do you know why you were given your name? Does it have a special meaning?

_____
_____
_____
_____
_____

What was your birth order among your siblings?

_____
_____
_____
_____
_____
_____

What stories have you been told about yourself as a baby?

_____
_____
_____
_____
_____
_____
_____
_____
_____

What are your earliest memories of your childhood?

_____
_____
_____
_____
_____
_____
_____
_____
_____
_____
_____
_____
_____
_____
_____
_____
_____

Do you consider your childhood happy? Why or why not?

_____

What were you like as a child?

_____

Describe the home(s) and neighborhood(s) in which you grew up.

___

Describe your family's economic conditions and the other factors that affected your lifestyle.

___

Tell about your brothers and sisters, as well as step-siblings, and your relationships with each of them when you were little.

The direction in which education starts a man will determine his future life.

Plato

Did you go to nursery school or kindergarten? What do you remember about it?

Describe your first elementary school. What was your first day there like?

What memories do you have about getting to and from school?

When you got home from school each day, who was there to greet you? What was the first thing you usually did after school?

Tell about your favorite or least favorite teachers.

_____
_____
_____
_____
_____
_____
_____
_____
_____
_____
_____
_____
_____
_____

What was your favorite subject? Why?

_____
_____
_____
_____

Did you ever receive an award or recognition for special achievement?

_____
_____
_____
_____
_____

Do you remember the occurrence of any significant historic event(s) during your elementary school days?

___

Which friends do you best remember and why?

___

What games and activities did you enjoy?

___

Tell about the first motion picture you ever saw.

What were your favorite radio and television shows?

Did you have any pets? What were they? What were their names? How important were they in your life?

Did you ever have a special place where you went to be alone?

What did you daydream about?

What were your favorite things to eat? Are there any smells, flavors, sounds, songs, etc. that bring back memories of your childhood?

What birthday do you remember most? Why?

_____
_____
_____
_____
_____
_____
_____
_____
_____

How did you spend your summers?

_____
_____
_____
_____
_____
_____
_____
_____

Where did your family go on vacations? Which is your most memorable vacation?

_____
_____
_____
_____
_____
_____
_____
_____

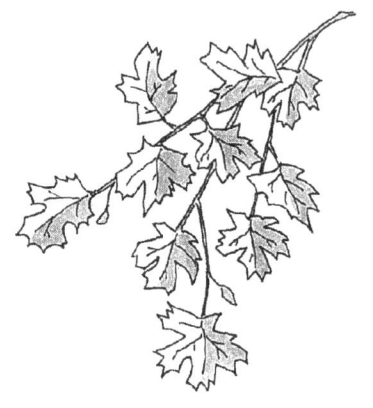

*Bring up a child
in the way he should go,
and when he is old
he will not depart from it.*

Proverbs 22:6

Describe how important religion was to your family when you were little?

What part did religion play in your social activities?

Which religious holidays were celebrated in your home? Describe.

What do you remember about any health epidemics?

Were you ever seriously ill when you were little?

Did you have any serious accidents as a child?

Did you experience a family tragedy during childhood? How did it affect you?

_____
_____
_____
_____
_____
_____
_____
_____
_____
_____
_____
_____
_____
_____
_____
_____

Did anything unusual or strange happen to you during your childhood?

_____
_____
_____
_____
_____
_____
_____
_____
_____
_____
_____
_____
_____
_____
_____

What were your greatest fears when you were a child?

Did you have any favorite relatives? How were they important to you?

Tell about the people who influenced you the most in your childhood.

What are the most memorable experiences you shared with your grandparents?

What is your saddest childhood memory?

Tell the story about something funny that happened during your childhood.

*There is always
one moment in childhood
when the door opens
and lets the future in.*

Graham Green

Tell the story about a frightening event from your childhood.

What is your happiest childhood memory?

What other memories would you like to share about your childhood?

Teen Years

In all likelihood, our teenage years were mostly a time of continuous anxiety. We were re-forming our personalities, seeking freedom from the ways of our childhood, and establishing new relationships with peers based on our emerging identities.

It seemed that the activities surrounding us at the time were chaotic and overwhelming. Still, we were compelled to shun guidance from our parents and to find our own way in this turmoil. Although we desperately needed their advice and attention, many of us systematically rejected it in our attempt to find our independence and self-sufficiency. More than anything, it seemed that we didn't want to be seen as being like our parents. We disobeyed and rebelled so we could feel our own autonomy.

If you were like most teens, the agony of self-consciousness and feelings of ineptitude in social situations added to the uncertainty, self-doubt and ambivalence of your teen years. Perhaps you were torn between wanting to have some stability and control over your life by holding on to the comfortable ways of the past and desiring strongly to establish your identity and your role in the real world. Although that world lay before you, maybe you felt it was on top of you as you attempted to meet the rising expectations of family, friends, and others around you.

Your thoughts, feelings and experiences during your teen years likely reflect how much you have in common with successive generations.

Adolescence is the age at which children stop asking questions because they know all the answers.

Jeanne Opalach

Describe the area – city, small town, farm – where you spent most of your teen years.

Describe yourself as a teenager. What things were important to you?

What do you remember most about your school experiences while a teenager?

Were you involved in extracurricular activities in high school?

What was your favorite subject? Why?

*A teacher affects eternity;
he can never tell
where his influence stops.*

Henry Brooks Adams

Did you have a favorite teacher in high school? How did she or he influence you?

_____
_____
_____
_____
_____
_____
_____
_____
_____
_____
_____
_____
_____
_____

Was religion an important part of your life during your teen years? Explain.

_____
_____
_____
_____
_____
_____
_____
_____
_____
_____
_____
_____
_____
_____

Describe any part-time jobs you had in your teen years.

What were your favorite leisure activities?

Describe your best friends during your teen years.

Where did you and your friends spend time and what did you do there?

*Dear friend whoever you are
take this kiss,
I give it especially to you,
do not forget me ...*

Walt Whitman

Tell about your first date and first kiss.

_____

Tell about your first steady boyfriend or girlfriend. How long did you go together?

_____

What were the most mischievous pranks you pulled?

What were the attitudes among teenagers about sex, smoking, drugs, and alcohol?

What kinds of things did you and your friends do on dates?

Did you attend your school dances or proms? With whom? Describe them.

What were some of the "fads" when you were a teenager?

Describe the hair and clothing styles that were popular.

What did you like best and least about your appearance as a teenager?

What slang expressions were popular during your teen years?

What kind of music was popular? What was your favorite song? Who was your favorite musical performer or band?

_____

What kinds of dances were popular during your teen years?

_____

What was your favorite motion picture? Why?

_____
_____
_____
_____
_____
_____
_____
_____

Describe your relationship with your parents. Were you able to communicate freely with them?

_____
_____
_____
_____
_____
_____
_____
_____
_____
_____
_____
_____
_____
_____
_____
_____
_____

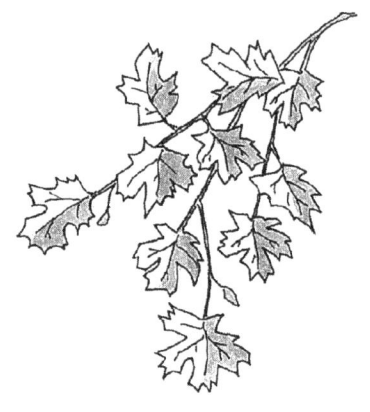

*Children have never been
very good at
listening to their elders,
but they have never failed
to imitate them.*

James Baldwin

How did you typically get in trouble with your parents? How were you punished?

Did you ever get in trouble at school? What happened?

Did you ever skip school? To do what?

Were you compatible with your siblings? Did you ever play tricks on them?

When did you get your first car? Did you pay for it or was it a gift? Describe it.

What did you do in summers when school was out?

If you moved during your teen years, how did you feel about leaving your friends and attending a different school?

Did you accomplish something in your teens of which you are very proud?

What was your greatest fear when you were a teenager?

To whom did you turn for advice? Why that person?

Whom did you admire the most as a teenager? Why?

Who influenced you most during your teen years? How?

Tell the story about something funny or embarrassing that happened to you as a teenager.

Did you have a nickname? What was it and how did you get it?

Who was leader of your country and what do you remember most about that person?

What was the most historic event that took place during "your generation"? How did it affect you?

What is the happiest memory you have of your teen years?

What is your most painful memory as a teenager?

When did you graduate from high school? What was your graduation ceremony like? How did you celebrate?

When did you move away from home and where did you go?

What was the hardest part of being a teenager?

Is there anything else you would like to share about your teen years?

Higher Education

Going to college was the first time many of us had extensive choices to make about what direction our lives would take. What we experienced in college went far beyond the world of academia. The college experience stimulated our creativity within an environment perhaps best suited to allow it to unfold. Intellectual growth was accompanied by personal growth. It was a time when we truly began to discover self and to form our own independent, personal identity. We established firm beliefs, a greater appreciation for past human achievements, a sense of the inter-dependency of people, and a willingness to work tirelessly to achieve self-established goals.

Your exposure to the diversity of perspectives in many new social relationships, your exploration of thoughts and theories, the deepening of bonds with other persons, and the "looking within" that occurred as you found your place in the world, helped you grow to some certainty and acceptance of what life had to offer. As you focused more and more on your future and your lifetime goals, your choices were greatly influenced by a heightened idealism at one extreme, and the almost casual turns occasioned by those you met on campus at the other.

Whether by choice or chance, your life's path began to unfold.

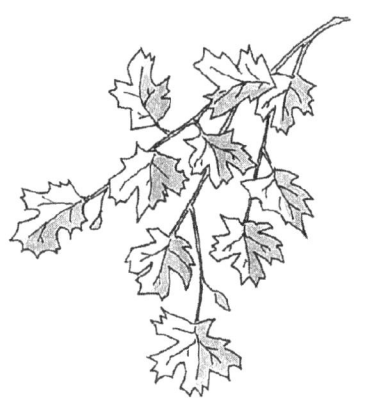

*Learning is not attained by chance;
It must be sought for with ardor
And attended to with diligence.*

Abigail Adams

Where did you go to college and why?

What was your major and why did you choose it?

Describe where you lived while at college.

Did you have to work during college? What did you do and how much was your pay?

_____
_____
_____
_____
_____
_____
_____
_____

Which professor(s) influenced your life and career the most? Explain.

_____
_____
_____
_____
_____
_____
_____
_____

How did college change you?

_____
_____
_____
_____
_____
_____
_____

If you joined a fraternity or sorority, which one? How did you like it? What was the initiation like?

Tell about your best friends in college.

Where did you go and what did you do to socialize?

_____
_____
_____
_____
_____
_____
_____
_____
_____

What were the fads and slang when you were in college?

_____
_____
_____
_____
_____
_____
_____
_____
_____

What was your favorite music and who were your favorite music artists?

_____
_____
_____
_____
_____
_____
_____
_____

Tell about your love relationships while in college.

Were you a serious student or did you play too much?

Tell about your happiest memory from college.

Tell about your most painful memory.

Tell about an amusing event that happened during college.

Did you ever get into trouble while attending college? For what? How were you punished?

What did you enjoy most about college?

Tell about your graduation and celebration.

What was the most foolish thing you did during college?

Of which of your college accomplishments are you the proudest?

The great aim of education is not knowledge but action.

Herbert Spencer

Is there anything else you would like to share about your college years?

Military

Ideally, the military services instill character, self-discipline, workplace skills, and leadership qualities in their members. While the military as a career has become a more and more appealing option to those who are so inclined, the military tradition of our country is based on the notion of the "citizen soldier". That is, more often than not, people take time out from their civilian life to don a uniform and serve their country and then return to mainstream society when their duty is over. For a time, they put aside their personal goals and dedicate themselves to the goals of the service they have entered.

The quality of military life can differ greatly among the various branches and assignments within each branch. Accordingly, the impact on spouse and family can vary greatly. Each experience is unique.

Whether during peace time or war time, your wearing of the uniform displayed your commitment to the service of your country. Your experiences and endeavors in this regard are of special significance to those whose freedoms you have helped preserve.

*The first virtue in a soldier
is endurance of fatigue;
courage is only the second virtue.*

Napoleon Bonaparte

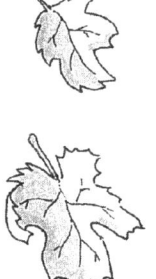

Did you enlist in the military or were you drafted? In what branch did you serve?

Where was your basic training and what was it like?

Where were you stationed and for how long? What was your specialty? Describe your living arrangements.

Where did you go and what did you do for rest and relaxation?

Were any of your children born while you were in the military? What was military family life like?

Describe your feelings and experiences about being apart from loved ones.

Were you ever in combat? Tell about some experiences.

Were you involved in or did you see anyone engage in tremendous acts of courage?

Did you win any medals or decorations? For what?

What was it like for you when the war ended?

Altogether, how long did you serve? What was your highest rank?

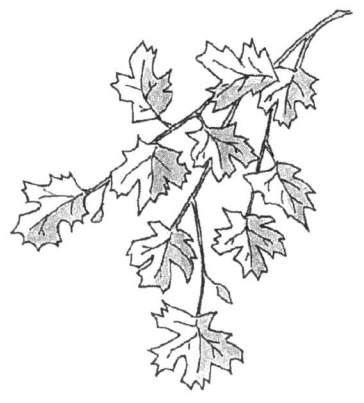

War never leaves a nation where it found it.

Edmund Burke

What did you do right after your military service?

What was the hardest adjustment you had to make returning to civilian life?

How was your life changed by being in the military?

Tell about your best friends in the service.

What are your most painful memories about military life?

What did you enjoy most about military life?

Is there anything else you would like to say about your military experience?

Independence, Work and Career

Obtaining our own independence meant stepping away, for the first time, from the security of our family. Instead of relying on our parents, we had to fend for ourselves. We became responsible – for everything. This was a tremendous challenge, and a very exhilarating time in our lives as we discovered previously unknown skills, stifled interests, and underdeveloped personality traits.

Although our parents' expectations still influenced our choice of work, most of us selected a certain career path because we felt we would enjoy the work involved. For better or for worse, our work established our identity in the eyes of many. To most people it represented, and still represents, "who we are".

To the extent that your career allowed you to do what you loved to do, new significance and meaning was provided in your life. Your work may have become the primary way you expressed yourself to the outside world. Your level of satisfaction with your work at different stages of your career probably mirrors your self-worth, emotional well-being, and general happiness at those times.

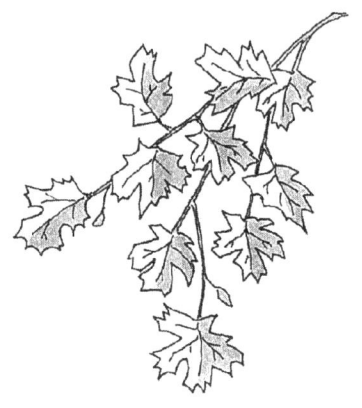

*First say to yourself
what you would be;
and then do
what you have to do.*

Epictetus

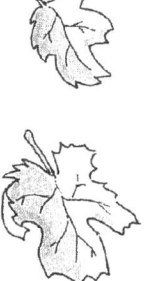

What did you do after high school, college, or military service?

In what part of the country did you live when you first left home? Why?

Describe what you were like when first "on your own".

___

How was your relationship with your family after you moved out?

___

What were your dreams and goals during your first years of independence?

___

Tell about your friends and the kinds of things you did together.

Tell about your love interests at this time.

*There is as much dignity
in tilling a field
as in writing a poem.*

Booker T. Washington

Who most influenced you in your early adulthood? Why or how?

Tell about your first job which enabled you to become self-supporting.

How greatly did your first job influence the development of your later career?

Did you ever own your own business? What was it and how did you get started?

What led you to your line of work or career?

_____

_____

_____

_____

_____

_____

_____

_____

_____

_____

_____

_____

_____

_____

Did you ever change your line of work or career? How many times? Why?

_____

_____

_____

_____

_____

_____

_____

_____

_____

_____

_____

_____

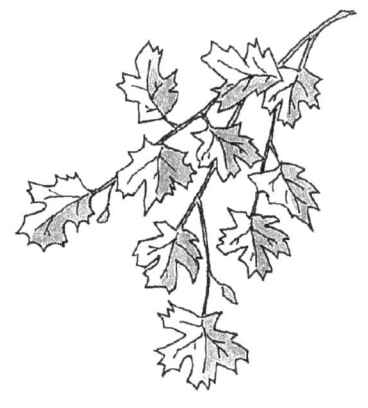

*I long to accomplish
a great and noble task,
but it is my chief duty
to accomplish small tasks
as if they were great and noble.*

Helen Keller

How did your level of education influence your career?

Tell about the high points in your career.

Did you ever have any major setbacks during your career? How did you cope?

Did you work primarily out of economic necessity or for personal fulfillment?

What has been your motivation to achieve or succeed in your career?

Do you have any interesting work-related stories to tell?

*Far and away
the best prize that life offers
is the chance to work hard
at work worth doing.*

Theodore Roosevelt

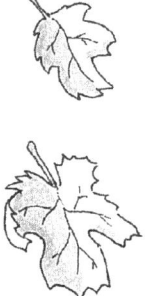

Of what accomplishments in your career are you the proudest?

If you had a mentor, who was it? Describe the guidance you were given.

If you could have changed careers to something completely different, what would it have been and why?

Is there anything else you would like to share about your work and career?

Love and Marriage

Love is our most powerful emotion. It plays the biggest part in our happiness. It can bring out the best in us and make us feel on top of the world. Our love relationships are some of the most important aspects of our lives. Falling in love is exciting and absorbing. We find a new energy. We become thoughtful, attentive and romantic.

From the intriguing stories about how you found the love(s) of your life, and what initially attracted you, to the adjustments and challenges you faced in a shared life, your experiences with love, more often than not, have had the greatest influence on the course of your actions.

Getting married was one of the most important decisions in your life. Marriage gave you the opportunity for complete personal fulfillment and the full expression of yourself through a dynamic and intimate partnership with another. You made commitments to your mate which reflected your self-established ideals for shared commitment, understanding, intimacy and love itself. Then you spent much of a lifetime working each day to achieve those ideals.

*The real marriage of true minds
is for any two people to possess a sense of humour
or irony pitched in exactly the same key,
so that their joint glances at any subject
cross like interarching searchlights.*

Edith Wharton

How did you meet your future spouse?

Describe what your future spouse was like and tell something about his or her background.

What was it about your future spouse that most attracted you?

What was your first date with your future spouse like?

What was your engagement proposal like?

What was your courtship like and how long did you know each other before you got married?

_____
_____
_____
_____
_____
_____
_____
_____
_____
_____
_____
_____

Give the date of your wedding and tell about the ceremony, the place, attire, decorations, etc. How old were you and your spouse?

_____
_____
_____
_____
_____
_____
_____
_____
_____
_____
_____
_____

Tell about your honeymoon.

What pet names did you and your spouse have for each other? How did you select them?

Tell about your first home together. What was the community like?

Do you have a favorite story about being newlyweds?

*Love seems the swiftest,
but it is the slowest of all growths.
No man or woman really knows
what perfect love is
until they have been married
a quarter of a century.*

Mark Twain

What was your first year of marriage like?

How did you get along with your in-laws?

What was the hardest adjustment you had to make that first year?

What things did you argue about most in the early years?

How did you and your significant other resolve conflict?

How important was religion in your marriage? Did you and your spouse attend religious services together?

Did you enjoy vacationing together? What was your favorite destination?

*A successful marriage requires
falling in love many times
with the same person.*

What were the hardest times in your marriage?

If you stayed together, what is the "glue" that kept you together?

What was your economic status during your early years of marriage?

Did you move often during your marriage? Where did you finally settle, and why?

What do you admire most about your spouse?

___

What do you admire least about your spouse?

___

What have you learned about your spouse over the years that you did not know when you married her or him?

___

If your marriage ended, tell about how it happened. How did you cope with it? How did it feel being single again?

If you married again, what was different about your subsequent marriage(s)?

Is there anything else you would like to share about your marriage(s)?

Parenthood

When we think back on ourselves as parents, most of us recognize that we were constantly engaged in a balancing act. The nurturing and raising of our children often interfered with our spousal relationship, our income-producing work, our connections with the rest of the world – in fact, our entire lives. Our intimate role in helping our children through their years of development is probably never paralleled.

Equipped with little or no experience and facing what seemed at the time like an overwhelming responsibility, we taught as we learned, doing our best and wondering why we couldn't do better. When all was over, most of us asked ourselves, "Did we measure up?" The truth is that virtually none of us could live up to our culture's institutionalized definition of the ideal parent who could be absolutely selfless and give to children according to their needs without any resentment, hesitation, or conflict. Most of us were still maturing as we raised our children.

Your parenting style was critical in your children's creation of their self-image. Your beliefs about life, your values, and your behavior towards your children and others in their presence during their formative years, help to explain your thoughts, feelings, and actions during that time, and their attitudes and behavior for many years that followed.

Children live what they learn.

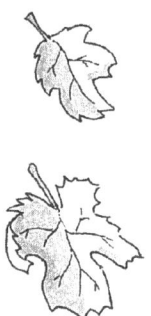

When and why did you make the decision to have children? How many did you "plan" to have?

___

What was the first pregnancy like? How, when and where did the birth occur?

___

How did your first child change your lifestyle? Was being a parent what you expected?

Give the names of all your children, their birthdates and any circumstances that made their births unusual. How did you choose each child's name?

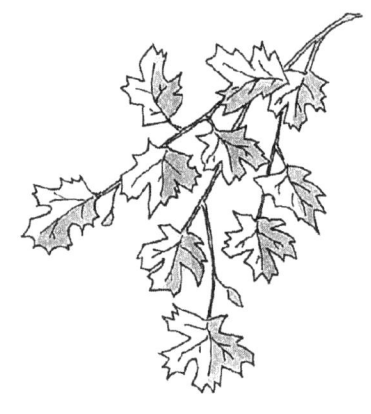

*There is no friendship,
no love,
like that of the parent
for the child.*

Christopher Pearse Cranch

Tell a story about each child's early years.

Did you have any special pet names or nicknames you used for your children? Why were they chosen?

Did your family move often? If so, how do you think it affected your children?

Describe the home(s) in which you raised your children. Where were they? Tell about each neighborhood and community.

Did you ever employ a nanny or guardian for your children? Tell about her or him.

How did your family celebrate holidays?

Describe a typical family activity or outing.

___

Did you take your children on family vacations? Tell about your favorite.

___

*If you want your children
to turn out well,
spend twice as much time with them,
and half as much money.*

Abigail Van Buren

Describe a typical family meal time.

_____

Did you and your children attend religious services together? How often? Explain.

_____

Did your children have any medical emergencies or serious illnesses?

What were your major concerns about your children as teenagers?

Describe the personalities of each of your children and your relationship with each.

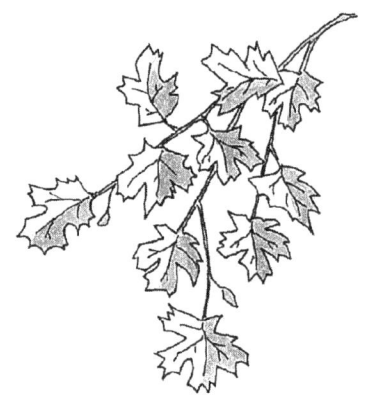

*The children despise their parents
until the age of forty,
when they suddenly become just like them,
thus preserving the system.*

Quentin Crewe

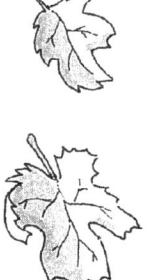

Can you share some memorable moments about each child's teen years?

Which child is most like you and which is most like your spouse? How?

Did any of your children have an exceptional talent?

Describe your parenting style, including discipline. Did it change over the years? How did it compare to your parents' style?

_____
_____
_____
_____
_____
_____
_____
_____
_____
_____
_____
_____

Did you and your spouse have any major differences about how to raise your children?

_____
_____
_____
_____
_____
_____
_____
_____
_____
_____
_____
_____

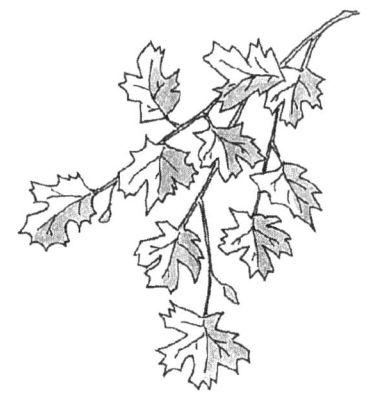

*There is just one way
to bring up a child
in the way he should go,
and that is
to travel that way yourself.*

Abraham Lincoln

If you were a stepparent, what were the most difficult aspects?

Have your parents played an important role in the lives of your children?

What is the proudest moment you had as a parent?

What is the worst part of being a parent?

What is the best part of being a parent?

What was it like for you when your children left home?

Is there anything else you would like to share about parenthood?

Middle Years

Mid-life is usually a time of transition, of major changes in our lives. We find ourselves readjusting our lifestyles and re-evaluating our priorities. Our children leave home. We may become widowed or divorced. We re-enter the work force, return to school, or take on other roles. We each find our own ways of adapting to these transitions. We make mistakes and we also achieve greater fulfillment and become stronger people.

Our place in the world of the future may become unclear to us. We can suffer regrets over things we have not done and anxieties about things we feel we must accomplish. It is a period during which we undergo a renewal of awareness, a flexibility to change with each new challenge and a desire to address our deepest personal issues which have festered with inattention.

Ideally, the triggering of this new awareness brought on by our middle years results in a positive transformation, in which we abandon the narrow life endeavors charted during our youth and are drawn toward contributing to universal good in the context of the broadest human issues of peace, justice, understanding, and dignity for all mankind.

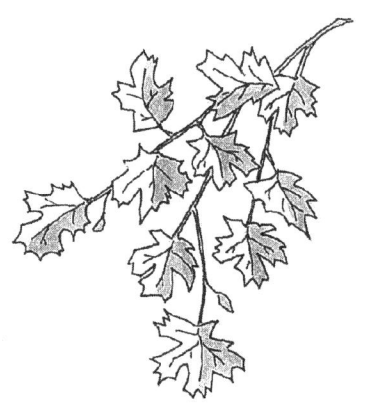

One of the hardest decisions in life is when to start middle age.

What were the most important things you had learned about life by the time you reached middle-age?

Between the ages of 40 and 65, what was the best year for you and why? The worst year and why?

When did you "discover" you were middle-aged?

How did you prefer to spend your leisure time?

How was your relationship with your children during these years?

What was your relationship with your parents like during these years?

Whoever in middle age attempts to realize
the wishes and hopes of his early youth
invariably deceives himself.
Each ten years of a man's life
has its own fortunes,
its own hopes, its own desires.

Goethe

Did your relationship with your significant other change in the middle years?

What were your strengths and weaknesses during this time?

Did you suffer any financial or emotional losses during your middle years? How did you deal with them?

What did you fear the most during the middle years?

Did you experience changes in your physical well-being? Did you have any surgeries?

If you had a mid-life crisis, at what age was it? Describe what you thought and felt. Did your life take a new direction?

The trick is growing up without growing old.

Casey Stengel

How did your values, goals and priorities change?

What is the most significant realization you came to during your middle years?

What do you believe to be your most important accomplishments in mid-life?

What was the best part of being middle-aged?

Is there anything else you would like to share about your middle-age years?

Golden Years

As a people, we are living longer than ever before. We have more time to live enjoyable, successful lives. We are freer to do what we want, when we want to do it, and to go where we want to go, when we want to go there, and it seems that we don't have to answer to anyone or justify our choices. This new freedom, coupled with the differing priorities that later life brings, provides the opportunity for personal growth unavailable to most people in the earlier stages of their lives.

Also, it seems that with extended age comes a greater accumulation of knowledge and wisdom which, when shared, can enable younger generations to reach their full potential more easily and to preserve the traditions of family and culture.

In these years, you constitute a vital link between the past and the present that can enhance future outcomes for those who follow you. Important for more than just historical and personal interest reasons, your golden years provide unique insight which will help your descendants embrace maturity in the most positive way, thereby living the longest, healthiest and happiest lives possible.

Getting old is better than the alternative.

W. E. Clyde

How did you feel upon becoming a senior citizen?

Have your senior years been like you always thought they would be? If not, how have they been different?

Tell about how and when you decided to retire?

Have you taken up any hobbies or interests after retiring?

Have you remained active throughout your senior years?

What misconceptions do people have about being a senior citizen?

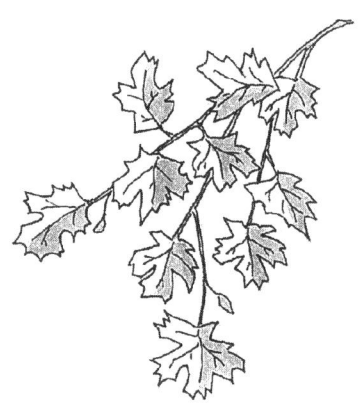

*With the ancient is wisdom;
and in length of years understanding.*

Job, The Old Testament

What is your favorite joke about the golden years?

Do you feel you have attained a certain wisdom with age?

Have you become emotionally stronger with age? Explain.

Have you lost many loved ones? If so, how have their losses affected you?

Have you remained healthy into your golden years?

What is the best part about being a senior citizen?

*If I'd known I was gonna live this long,
I'd have taken better care of myself.*

Eubie Blake

What is the worst part about being a senior citizen?

What changes should be made to benefit senior citizens?

Have you ever been discriminated against or treated unfairly because of age?

Does being a senior offer any special opportunities or privileges?

Do you feel people today give seniors the respect they deserve? Explain.

During your golden years, have you played an important role in the lives of your grandchildren?

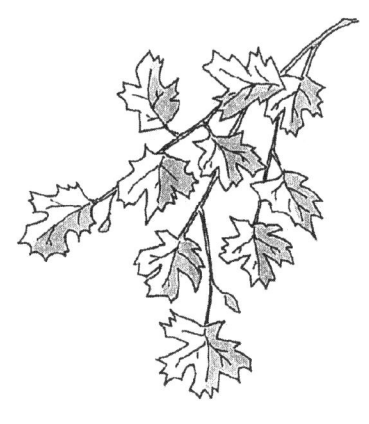

*The first 40 years of life gives us the text;
the next 30 supply the commentary.*

Arthur Schopenhauer

Are any of your looks, personality traits, or talents evident in your grandchildren?

Is there anything else you would like to say about your golden years?

Ethnic Heritage

The ethnicity of any group of people comes into being through the dynamic interaction of an infinite number of variables which occur often over generations. The ethnic affinity of a population seemingly is in a state of constant change. The definition of anyone's ethnic ancestry is at best elusive and too often completely lost, if not pointedly studied from generation to generation.

More than ever immigrants are settling in countries other than their own homeland. They bring with them unique contributions to the cultures of their adopted nations. The variety of races and ethnicities which make up many societies is wide indeed, and the defining attributes of each of these "different" groups of people can vary greatly.

When others think of your ethnic group, they may think of its most obvious characteristics, such as its food, religion, language, family structures, mode of dress, etc. Less apparent to most people are the differences and the deepest values within its culture, which greatly influence the makeup of any individual member. Likewise, an understanding of the attitudes of others toward persons of your ethnicity is essential to an accurate perspective on your life.

*There's a magical tie
to the land of our home,
which the heart cannot break,
though the footsteps may roam.*

Eliza Cook

What is your ethnic origin?

What does your ethnic and cultural background mean to you?

What are the most important holidays celebrated as part of your ethnic heritage? Tell about them.

Tell about some traditions and rituals of your ethnic group and what they mean to you.

Describe the foods common to your ethnic group.

How do you feel about maintaining a strong identity in your ethnic and cultural heritage?

Is a certain religious denomination associated with your ethnic group? Describe a typical worship service.

Did you have a ceremonial rite of passage?

What makes you proudest to be a member of your ethnic group?

What contributions have members of your ethnic group made to the world?

Which famous members of your ethnic group do you admire the most? Why?

Have you ever been to your ancestral land? Tell about your trip and what it meant to you.

When you were growing up, what were the things your parents told you about people outside your ethnic group?

_____

How do you feel about marriage to people outside your ethnic group?

_____

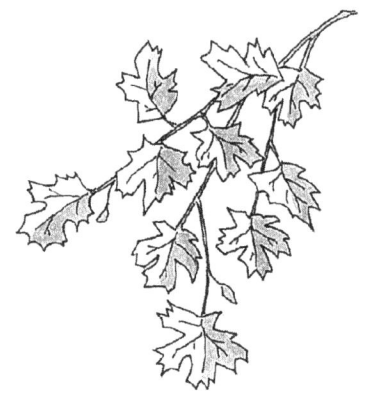

Prejudice is a burden that confuses the past, threatens the future and renders the present inaccessible...

Maya Angelou

From ALL GOD'S CHILDREN NEED TRAVELING SHOES by Maya Angelou.
Copyright © 1986 by Maya Angelou. Reprinted by permission of Random House, Inc.

Tell about the first time you became aware of ethnic prejudice.

Is there a particular incident of ethnic prejudice that stands out in your memory?

What stories have you been told by your parents or grandparents about incidents of ethnic prejudice?

_____

What do you believe causes ethnic prejudice? What could be done to get rid of it?

_____

How have attitudes and the quality of life changed with regard to your ethnic group in your lifetime?

What message about being a member of your ethnic group would you like to leave for posterity?

Men are not superior by reason of the accidents of race or color. They are superior who have the best heart...

Robert G. Ingersoll

What else would you like to say about your ethnicity?

Regrets, Mistakes, Milestones and Turning Points

The choices we make at each fork in the road affect us for the balance of our lives. While even our smallest decisions reflect who we are at the time and who we will ultimately become, there are major events and choices we can point to as having greatly influenced the course of our lives.

There are personal and professional accomplishments which give us great pride or which make us feel that we have truly contributed something of value to mankind. There are things we wanted to do but never did. There are things we wish we had done differently.

By giving your perspective on the most significant occurrences in your life, you can share with your descendants the wisdom you have gained. Your interpretations of these events cannot serve as complete road maps on how others should live their lives. However, the markers which have charted your journey can assist your children and their children in finding their way to the fullest expression of their own potential as human beings.

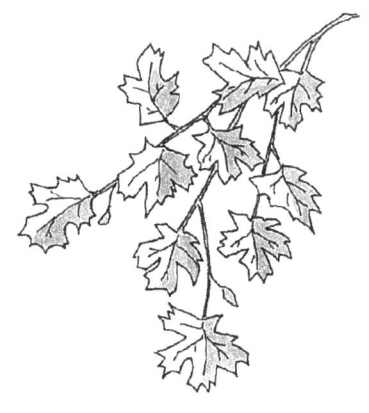

When to the sessions of sweet silent thought
I summon up remembrance of things past,
I sigh the lack of many a thing I sought,
And with old woes new wail my dear Time's waste...

William Shakespeare

What is the biggest mistake you ever made?

What is the smartest decision you ever made?

Is there something you have always dreamed of doing but never did?

What have you feared that has kept you from doing all that you wanted to do?

Do you have a talent or special gift you have not used?

What is the nicest thing you've ever done for someone else?

Did you ever put something extremely important off until it was too late?

Did you ever do something in spite of everyone's advice not to do it? What was it and how did it turn out?

What was the most important decision you ever had to make? Do you feel you made the right decision?

Is there any particular incident in your life that changed everything? For better or worse? Explain.

Footfalls echo in the memory
Down the passage which we did not take
Towards the door we never opened
Into the rose garden.

T. S. Elliot

Where have you always wanted to go but never have?

What dreams have you had during your lifetime? Have any become a reality?

Have you had a close brush with death or other spiritual experience that changed your life?

If you have had or still have a terminal illness, how has it changed your life?

Have you ever saved someone's life? Tell the story.

Has anyone ever saved your life? Tell the story.

*Into each life
some rain must fall,
Some days must be
dark and dreary.*

Henry Wadsworth Longfellow

Has someone important in your life died before you had the opportunity to tell them something? Who was it and what would you have said?

When in your life were you hurt the most?

Have you ever had a feud with someone you love that went on too long?

Have you ever been involved in a destructive relationship?

Have you ever been the victim of a "con artist"?

What act or person has been a source of great inspiration in your life?

Describe the funniest, silliest, or most embarrassing event(s) in your adult life.

Describe the happiest event(s) in your adult life.

Have you been a victim of a violent crime? Explain what happened and how you dealt with it.

_____
_____
_____
_____
_____
_____
_____
_____
_____
_____
_____
_____
_____
_____
_____

Were you ever involved in a major natural disaster?

_____
_____
_____
_____
_____
_____
_____
_____
_____
_____
_____
_____

Have you ever witnessed a seemingly supernatural event?

If you could change the way you handled your most significant relationship, what would you do differently?

If you could change how you raised your children, what would you do differently?

If you have had an addiction, what caused it and what has been its impact on your life and the lives of your family and friends?

What are the best and worst business decisions you ever made and how did they affect your life?

Were you ever destitute? How did you overcome it?

At this point in your life, of which of your accomplishments are you the proudest?

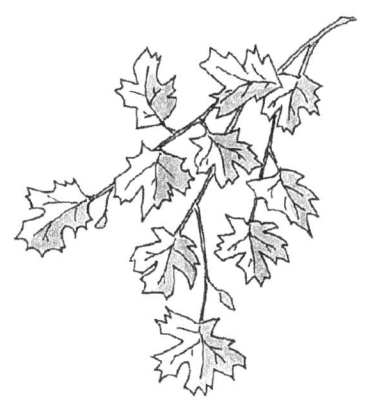

I shall be telling this with a sigh
Somewhere ages and ages hence:
Two roads diverged in a wood, and
I took the one less traveled by,
And that has made all the difference.

Robert Frost

If you knew it was impossible to fail, what would you set out to accomplish now?

What do you know now that you wish you had known when you were younger?

What period in your life did you enjoy most? Why?

If you could live your entire life over again, what would you do differently?

Beliefs, Values, Lessons and Advice

We all have values and beliefs which make up our view of the world. Some of us may see it as dangerous or ruthless, while others may see it as a good place where we can learn important lessons.

We all have different perspectives of what is real and yet we each tend to believe our view is the correct one. We construct our beliefs from direct experience. Our beliefs give our lives meaning. Our beliefs tell us when to feel fear, happiness, pain, etc. They determine our attitudes and behavior and influence our relationships, health, and lifestyles. Truly, we create our own reality by what we believe.

What you like and dislike, what is right and wrong to you, and so forth, are determined by your belief system, which is based on your perspective of what has happened in your life. Your reality reflects the lessons you have learned, and dictates the best advice you have for others.

*The purpose of life
is a life of purpose.*

Robert Byrne

What is the meaning of life?

What do you believe is a real mystery of life?

Explain your deepest values.

What advice do you have about getting through difficult times and coping with change?

What advice can you give regarding college and higher education?

Do you have any advice on choosing a career?

*As ye would that men should do to you,
do ye also to them likewise.*

Luke 6:31

What advice do you have for getting along with others?

What are the elements of real friendship?

*We may give advice,
but we cannot give conduct.*

Benjamin Franklin

How do you feel about abortion?

How do you feel about the death penalty?

Do you believe that the media have too much influence?

What quality do you consider most important in making a marriage work?

What advice do you have regarding divorce and remarriage?

What advice do you have on parenting?

What is your religious preference? What are the basic principles of your religion?

Have you changed your religion during your lifetime? Why?

What does God mean to you?

Are there some beliefs you have had but have given up? Why?

What are some of your favorite religious verses?

If you could ask one question of God, what would it be?

*Prayer is the contemplation
of the facts of life
from the highest point of view.*

Ralph Waldo Emerson

How often do you pray? What is the reason for prayer?

Have you become more spiritual as you've gotten older?

Do you believe in angels? Who or what are they?

Do you believe in miracles?

Do you believe humans have souls? If so, what is a soul?

Do you believe in an afterlife? What do you think it is like?

*God will not look you over
for medals, degrees,
or diplomas,
but for scars.*

Elbert Hubbard

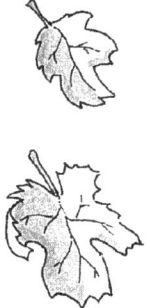

What is the most mystifying experience you've had?

What can young people learn from their elders?

Who is the wisest person you've ever met? In what way?

Why do we experience pain?

What brings happiness?

If you had only one week left to live, what would you do?

_____

Have you made peace with everyone important in your life? Explain.

_____

What is the most important gift we can give another human being?

What is the hardest lesson you've ever had to learn?

What do you feel has been your purpose in life?

Is it more important to plan for the future or to live in the present?

Write your epitaph.

How Life Has Changed

During the 20th century, technological and social changes have altered our lives more dramatically than at any other time in recorded history. Day-to-day living has been impacted tremendously by advances in medical technology, new thinking about education, greater access to the information highway, ethnic and cultural influences, the spread of industrialization, the failures of socialist experiments and the worldwide rise of market economies. These and other factors affect the way we think and feel from moment to moment, probably more than we really know.

You have your own views of the fluctuating structures of family life, relationships between men and women, the ways society views youth and the aged, the changing face of the work force, and the political and social trends and institutions of the greater society. Your personal recollections of and views about the changes you have seen can illuminate the sweeping events of your generation as well as the more intimate unfolding of your personal life.

There is nothing permanent except change.

Heraclitus

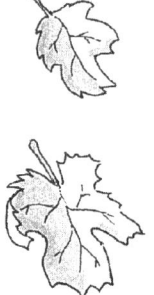

What are the most positive changes you have seen during your lifetime?

What are the most negative changes you have seen during your lifetime?

How have roles for women changed?

How have attitudes about marriage and family changed?

How have sexual mores changed?

What changes have you witnessed in attitudes about race, culture, ethnic differences, skin color, etc.?

What changes have occurred in the types of work people do?

Is today's younger generation very different from the young people of your generation? Have their values changed for better or worse?

What advantages do the youth of today have that you didn't have?

What is more difficult about growing up today than when you were growing up?

How have attitudes toward education changed?

How have salaries and the cost of living changed over the years?

How has housing changed?

How has the overall quality of life changed?

How have national and world politics and economics changed?

_____
_____
_____
_____
_____
_____
_____
_____
_____
_____
_____
_____
_____
_____
_____

Have there been any significant medical advances or cures in your lifetime?

_____
_____
_____
_____
_____
_____
_____
_____
_____
_____
_____
_____

How have modes of transportation changed?

What changes have you seen in forms of communication?

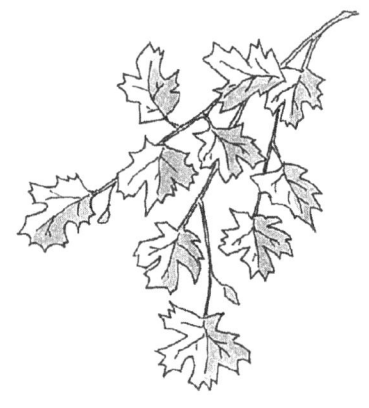

There has always been a food processor in the kitchen, but once upon a time, she was usually called, the missus, or Mom.

Sue Berkman

What "modern conveniences" have affected your lifestyle the most?

What inventions have had the greatest impact on mankind?

What other major technological changes have you seen?

How has the rising influence of mass media affected our society and the world at large?

What trends do you think will most change the course of our future?

Are there any other changes you view as significant?

Now

After all that has gone before, where have we arrived? Who are we and what is our purpose – right now? What are our present intentions and desires? Are we experiencing the freedom, security, power, happiness, well-being, satisfaction, respect, peace of mind, success and love that we dreamed of our whole life? Or do we feel fearful, angry, guilty, resentful, dissatisfied, unhappy, or unloved?

Who you are now is the sum total of all the years you have lived, the experiences you have had during those years, the influences of the people who have been in your life, the happiness you have enjoyed, the sorrow you have endured. You are the sum total of all that living – what you came away with. You are how you see the world. You are what you have adapted to. You are what you have reacted to. You are exactly what you have chosen to become.

*If you want to identify me,
ask me not where I live,
or what I like to eat,
or how I comb my hair,
but ask me what I am living for, in detail,
and ask me what I think
is keeping me from living fully
for the thing I want to live for.*

What is your name and age today? If different from your birth name, how did your name change?

_____
_____
_____
_____
_____
_____
_____
_____
_____
_____
_____
_____
_____
_____

Are you single, married, divorced, or widowed? Who is your significant other or the most important person in your life?

_____
_____
_____
_____
_____
_____
_____
_____
_____

Where and with whom do you live? Describe your living conditions.

What are you living your life for now? What are your personal priorities?

How is your health?

Do you have any "pet peeves"?

Describe your social life. Who are your friends? What do you do for fun?

What are your greatest personal concerns?

Where do you stand politically?

What concerns you most about what is going on in the world?

From whom do you feel you have learned the most about life? Explain.

Does religion play a role in your life?

Describe the spiritual you. Do you have "peace of mind"? Why or why not?

_____
_____
_____
_____
_____
_____
_____
_____
_____
_____
_____
_____
_____
_____

Describe the intellectual you.

_____
_____
_____
_____
_____
_____
_____
_____
_____
_____
_____

What do you see as your best qualities and strengths? For what are you complimented the most?

_____
_____
_____
_____
_____
_____
_____
_____
_____
_____
_____
_____
_____
_____

What gives you the greatest joy?

_____
_____
_____
_____
_____
_____
_____
_____
_____
_____

When are you saddest?

How do you deal with things you can't change? How do you handle stress?

*The thoughts we choose to think
are the tools we use
to paint the canvas of our lives.*

By what basic philosophy do you live?

What do you feel your greatest contribution to life has been?

What plans and goals do you have for the future?

How do you hope to be remembered?

What else would you like to say about who you are now?

Favorites

We all have preferences. Who knows what makes each of us have different tastes in clothes, entertainment, food, colors, etc.? Your preferences are interesting and intriguing and may tell volumes about you.

I'd rather have roses on my table than diamonds on my neck.

Emma Goldman

Tell what and why about your favorite ...

Book

___

Song

___

Movie

___

Color

___

Food

___

Gift

___

Flower

Holiday

Actor and Actress

Joke

Singer

_____
_____
_____
_____

Type of Music

_____
_____
_____
_____

Sports Team

_____
_____
_____
_____

Television Program

_____
_____
_____
_____

Perfume or cologne

_____
_____
_____

Author

_____
_____
_____
_____

*There are few hours in life
more agreeable than afternoon tea.*

Henry James

Season

Recipe

Leisure Activity

Political Leader

Hero

Artist

Pick-Me-Up

Quote

Snack Food

Vacation Spot

Family tradition

Family get-together

Special Questions

This chapter may include questions entered by the one who has given you this book, which indicates their importance to the giver. Likewise, issues about which you feel strongly, recollections and experiences that are of particular significance to you and that have not been covered elsewhere in this book, special messages to certain people, and secrets which you feel must be told, can be addressed in this chapter.

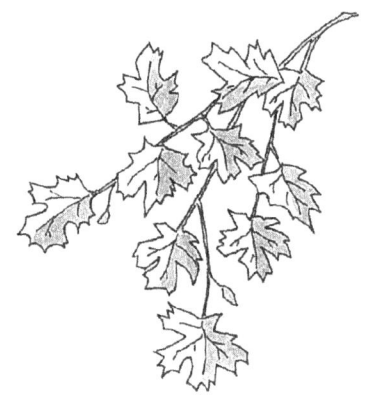

If you cannot get rid of the family skeleton, you may as well make it dance.

George Bernard Shaw

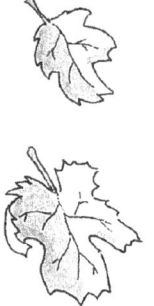

What is the most important thing you want your family and friends to know about you?

Are there any misconceptions about you that you want to set straight?

Is there an issue you feel strongly about but have kept to yourself?

Are there any family or personal secrets you want to share?

*The farther backwards you can look,
the farther forward you are likely to see.*

Sir Winston Churchill

Continuation Pages

FAMILY TREE

MOTHER'S Side of the Family

Maternal Great Grandmother: _____

Date of birth: _____ Where: _____

Maternal Great Grandfather: _____

Date of birth: _____ Where _____

Paternal Great Grandmother: _____

Date of birth: _____ Where _____

Paternal Great Grandfather: _____

Date of birth: _____ Where _____

Grandmother: _____

Date of birth: _____ Where _____

Grandfather: _____

Date of birth: _____

Mother: _____

Date of birth: _____ Where _____

FATHER'S Side of the Family

Paternal Great Grandmother: _____

Date of birth: _____ Where: _____

Paternal Great Grandfather: _____

Date of birth: _____ Where _____

Maternal Great Grandmother: _____

Date of birth: _____ Where _____

Maternal Great Grandfather: _____

Date of birth: _____ Where _____

Grandmother: _____

Date of birth: _____ Where _____

Grandfather: _____

Date of birth: _____ Where _____

Father: _____

Date of birth: _____ Where _____

Brothers and Sisters

Name:　　　　　　　　　Birthday:　　　　　　　　　Died:

Immediate Family

Spouse: _____

Birthday: _____ Where: _____

Date of our marriage: _____ Where: _____

        Children: Birthday: Died:

Grandchildren

Name: Birthday:

Favorite Photographs and Mementos

This chapter is for attaching your favorite photographs of yourself, your family, your friends, your pets, or anything that you cherish. Also, attach letters, writings, documents, awards, birth certificates or anything of value you want to keep for posterity.

It is suggested that you cross-index each photograph or memento by writing the following underneath each:

"See ('first', 'second', etc.) answer on Page (page no.)."

and by writing the following underneath the corresponding answer:

"See ('photograph' or other item) on Page (page no.)."

379

Green grows the Spring,
and Autumn gold,
Whilst in between
A story's told.

Pamela and Stephen Pavuk

For information on *The Story of a Lifetime: A Keepsake of Personal Memoirs* and other books by Pamela and Stephen Pavuk, contact TriAngel Publishers, Inc. by calling 1-877-313-1444 or 1-800-579-1869, by facsimile at 1-888-874-2643, or by visiting www.thestoryofalifetime.com on the World Wide Web.

Other books by Pamela and Stephen Pavuk include:

Sharing a Lifetime: A Keepsake of Wedding Memoirs (TriAngel)

Meals and Memories: A Keepsake of Family Dining Traditions (TriAngel)